The

Kitchen Witch's

Culinary Concoctions

Katharine Rose

Brock Haus Press

The Kitchen Witch's Culinary Concoctions | Katharine Rose
ISBN: ISBN: 978-1-7340926-2-2

A Kitchen Witch's Blessing

Blessed be this kitchen of Air, Fire, Water, and Earth. Be warmed by the Sacred Light of the Goddess and God. May all that is created here by means both magickal and mundane, bring nourishment, healing, sustenance and cause harm to none. With Love, Peace, Joy and Magick, be now and always filled.

So mote it be!

RECIPE FOR _____

CULINARY CONCOCTION

CASTING SPELL FOR

_____

SERVES _____

PREP TIME _____

TOTAL TIME _____

OVEN TEMP _____

INGREDIENTS

_____

_____

_____

_____

_____

_____

_____

DIRECTIONS

_____

_____

_____

_____

_____

_____

_____

_____

INVOCATION

INVOCATION

"So Mote It Be"

RECIPE FOR _____

CULINARY CONCOCTION

CASTING SPELL FOR

_____

SERVES _____

PREP TIME _____

TOTAL TIME _____

OVEN TEMP _____

INGREDIENTS

_____

_____

_____

_____

_____

_____

DIRECTIONS

_____

_____

_____

_____

_____

_____

_____

_____

_____

INVOCATION

INVOCATION

"SO MOTE IT BE"

RECIPE FOR _____

CULINARY CONCOCTION

CASTING SPELL FOR

_____

SERVES _____

PREP TIME _____

TOTAL TIME _____

OVEN TEMP _____

INGREDIENTS

_____

_____

_____

_____

_____

_____

_____

DIRECTIONS

INVOCATION

INVOCATION

"SO MOTE IT BE"

RECIPE FOR _____

CULINARY CONCOCTION

CASTING SPELL FOR

_____

SERVES _____

PREP TIME _____

TOTAL TIME _____

OVEN TEMP _____

INGREDIENTS

_____

_____

_____

_____

_____

_____

_____

DIRECTIONS

_____

_____

_____

_____

_____

_____

_____

_____

INVOCATION

INVOCATION

"SO MOTE IT BE"

RECIPE FOR _____

CULINARY CONCOCTION

CASTING SPELL FOR

_____

SERVES _____

PREP TIME _____

TOTAL TIME _____

OVEN TEMP _____

INGREDIENTS

_____

_____

_____

_____

_____

_____

_____

DIRECTIONS

INVOCATION

INVOCATION

"SO MOTE IT BE"

RECIPE FOR _____

CULINARY CONCOCTION

CASTING SPELL FOR

_____

SERVES _____

PREP TIME _____

TOTAL TIME _____

OVEN TEMP _____

INGREDIENTS

_____
_____
_____
_____
_____
_____
_____

DIRECTIONS

_____
_____
_____
_____
_____
_____
_____
_____

INVOCATION

INVOCATION

"SO MOTE IT BE"

RECIPE FOR _____

CULINARY CONCOCTION

CASTING SPELL FOR

_____

SERVES _____

PREP TIME _____

TOTAL TIME _____

OVEN TEMP _____

INGREDIENTS

_____

_____

_____

_____

_____

_____

_____

DIRECTIONS

_____

_____

_____

_____

_____

_____

_____

_____

_____

INVOCATION

INVOCATION

"SO MOTE IT BE"

RECIPE FOR _____

CULINARY CONCOCTION

CASTING SPELL FOR

_____

SERVES _____

PREP TIME _____

TOTAL TIME _____

OVEN TEMP _____

INGREDIENTS

_____

_____

_____

_____

_____

_____

_____

DIRECTIONS

INVOCATION

INVOCATION

"SO MOTE IT BE"

RECIPE FOR _____

CULINARY CONCOCTION

CASTING SPELL FOR

_____

SERVES _____

PREP TIME _____

TOTAL TIME _____

OVEN TEMP _____

INGREDIENTS

_____

_____

_____

_____

_____

_____

DIRECTIONS

INVOCATION

INVOCATION

"SO MOTE IT BE"

RECIPE FOR _____

CULINARY CONCOCTION

CASTING SPELL FOR

_____

SERVES _____

PREP TIME _____

TOTAL TIME _____

OVEN TEMP _____

INGREDIENTS

_____

_____

_____

_____

_____

_____

_____

DIRECTIONS

INVOCATION

INVOCATION

"SO MOTE IT BE"

RECIPE FOR _____

CULINARY CONCOCTION

CASTING SPELL FOR

_____

SERVES _____

PREP TIME _____

TOTAL TIME _____

OVEN TEMP _____

INGREDIENTS

_____

_____

_____

_____

_____

_____

_____

DIRECTIONS

_____

_____

_____

_____

_____

_____

_____

_____

INVOCATION

INVOCATION

"SO MOTE IT BE"

RECIPE FOR _____

CULINARY CONCOCTION

CASTING SPELL FOR

_____

SERVES _____

PREP TIME _____

TOTAL TIME _____

OVEN TEMP _____

INGREDIENTS

_____

_____

_____

_____

_____

_____

_____

DIRECTIONS

_____

_____

_____

_____

_____

_____

_____

_____

INVOCATION

INVOCATION

"SO MOTE IT BE"

RECIPE FOR _____

CULINARY CONCOCTION

CASTING SPELL FOR

_____

SERVES _____

PREP TIME _____

TOTAL TIME _____

OVEN TEMP _____

INGREDIENTS

_____

_____

_____

_____

_____

_____

DIRECTIONS

_____

_____

_____

_____

_____

_____

_____

_____

INVOCATION

INVOCATION

"SO MOTE IT BE"

RECIPE FOR _____

CULINARY CONCOCTION

CASTING SPELL FOR

_____

SERVES _____

PREP TIME _____

TOTAL TIME _____

OVEN TEMP _____

INGREDIENTS

_____

_____

_____

_____

_____

_____

DIRECTIONS

_____

_____

_____

_____

_____

_____

_____

_____

INVOCATION

INVOCATION

"SO MOTE IT BE"

RECIPE FOR _____

CULINARY CONCOCTION

CASTING SPELL FOR

_____

SERVES _____

PREP TIME _____

TOTAL TIME _____

OVEN TEMP _____

INGREDIENTS

_____

_____

_____

_____

_____

_____

_____

DIRECTIONS

_____

_____

_____

_____

_____

_____

_____

_____

INVOCATION

INVOCATION

"So Mote it Be"

RECIPE FOR _____

CULINARY CONCOCTION

CASTING SPELL FOR

_____

SERVES _____

PREP TIME _____

TOTAL TIME _____

OVEN TEMP _____

INGREDIENTS

_____

_____

_____

_____

_____

_____

_____

DIRECTIONS

_____

_____

_____

_____

_____

_____

_____

_____

INVOCATION

INVOCATION

"SO MOTE IT BE"

RECIPE FOR _____

CULINARY CONCOCTION

CASTING SPELL FOR

_____

SERVES _____

PREP TIME _____

TOTAL TIME _____

OVEN TEMP _____

INGREDIENTS

_____

_____

_____

_____

_____

_____

_____

DIRECTIONS

_____

_____

_____

_____

_____

_____

_____

_____

_____

INVOCATION

INVOCATION

"SO MOTE IT BE"

RECIPE FOR _____

CULINARY CONCOCTION

CASTING SPELL FOR

_____

SERVES _____

PREP TIME _____

TOTAL TIME _____

OVEN TEMP _____

INGREDIENTS

_____

_____

_____

_____

_____

_____

_____

DIRECTIONS

_____

_____

_____

_____

_____

_____

_____

_____

_____

INVOCATION

INVOCATION

"SO MOTE IT BE"

RECIPE FOR _____

CULINARY CONCOCTION

CASTING SPELL FOR

_____

SERVES _____

PREP TIME _____

TOTAL TIME _____

OVEN TEMP _____

INGREDIENTS

_____

_____

_____

_____

_____

_____

_____

DIRECTIONS

INVOCATION

INVOCATION

"So Mote It Be"

RECIPE FOR _____

CULINARY CONCOCTION

CASTING SPELL FOR

_____

SERVES _____

PREP TIME _____

TOTAL TIME _____

OVEN TEMP _____

INGREDIENTS

_____

_____

_____

_____

_____

_____

_____

DIRECTIONS

INVOCATION

INVOCATION

"SO MOTE IT BE"

RECIPE FOR

CULINARY CONCOCTION

CASTING SPELL FOR

_____

SERVES _____
PREP TIME _____
TOTAL TIME _____
OVEN TEMP _____

INGREDIENTS

_____
_____
_____
_____
_____
_____
_____

DIRECTIONS

INVOCATION

INVOCATION

"SO MOTE IT BE"

RECIPE FOR _____

CULINARY CONCOCTION

CASTING SPELL FOR

_____

SERVES _____

PREP TIME _____

TOTAL TIME _____

OVEN TEMP _____

INGREDIENTS

_____

_____

_____

_____

_____

_____

_____

DIRECTIONS

_____

_____

_____

_____

_____

_____

_____

_____

INVOCATION

INVOCATION

"So Mote It Be"

RECIPE FOR _____

CULINARY CONCOCTION

CASTING SPELL FOR

_____

SERVES _____

PREP TIME _____

TOTAL TIME _____

OVEN TEMP _____

INGREDIENTS

_____

_____

_____

_____

_____

_____

DIRECTIONS

INVOCATION

INVOCATION

"SO MOTE IT BE"

RECIPE FOR _____

CULINARY CONCOCTION

CASTING SPELL FOR

_____

SERVES _____

PREP TIME _____

TOTAL TIME _____

OVEN TEMP _____

INGREDIENTS

_____

_____

_____

_____

_____

_____

_____

DIRECTIONS

_____

_____

_____

_____

_____

_____

_____

_____

INVOCATION

INVOCATION

"SO MOTE IT BE"

RECIPE FOR _____

CULINARY CONCOCTION

CASTING SPELL FOR

_____

SERVES _____

PREP TIME _____

TOTAL TIME _____

OVEN TEMP _____

INGREDIENTS

_____

_____

_____

_____

_____

_____

_____

DIRECTIONS

_____

_____

_____

_____

_____

_____

_____

_____

_____

INVOCATION

INVOCATION

"SO MOTE IT BE"

RECIPE FOR _____

CULINARY CONCOCTION

CASTING SPELL FOR

_____

SERVES _____

PREP TIME _____

TOTAL TIME _____

OVEN TEMP _____

INGREDIENTS

_____

_____

_____

_____

_____

_____

_____

DIRECTIONS

_____

_____

_____

_____

_____

_____

_____

_____

INVOCATION

INVOCATION

"SO MOTE IT BE"

RECIPE FOR _____

CULINARY CONCOCTION

CASTING SPELL FOR

_____

SERVES _____

PREP TIME _____

TOTAL TIME _____

OVEN TEMP _____

INGREDIENTS

_____

_____

_____

_____

_____

_____

_____

DIRECTIONS

_____

_____

_____

_____

_____

_____

_____

_____

_____

INVOCATION

INVOCATION

"SO MOTE IT BE"

RECIPE FOR _____

CULINARY CONCOCTION

CASTING SPELL FOR

_____

SERVES _____

PREP TIME _____

TOTAL TIME _____

OVEN TEMP _____

INGREDIENTS

_____

_____

_____

_____

_____

_____

_____

DIRECTIONS

_____

_____

_____

_____

_____

_____

_____

_____

_____

INVOCATION

INVOCATION

"So Mote it Be"

RECIPE FOR _____

CULINARY CONCOCTION

CASTING SPELL FOR

_____

SERVES _____

PREP TIME _____

TOTAL TIME _____

OVEN TEMP _____

INGREDIENTS

_____

_____

_____

_____

_____

_____

DIRECTIONS

INVOCATION

INVOCATION

"SO MOTE IT BE"

RECIPE FOR _____

CULINARY CONCOCTION

CASTING SPELL FOR

_____

SERVES _____

PREP TIME _____

TOTAL TIME _____

OVEN TEMP _____

INGREDIENTS

_____

_____

_____

_____

_____

_____

DIRECTIONS

INVOCATION

INVOCATION

"SO MOTE IT BE"

RECIPE FOR _____

CULINARY CONCOCTION

CASTING SPELL FOR

_____

SERVES _____

PREP TIME _____

TOTAL TIME _____

OVEN TEMP _____

INGREDIENTS

_____

_____

_____

_____

_____

_____

_____

DIRECTIONS

_____

_____

_____

_____

_____

_____

_____

_____

INVOCATION

INVOCATION

"So MOTE IT BE"

RECIPE FOR _____

CULINARY CONCOCTION

CASTING SPELL FOR

_____

SERVES _____

PREP TIME _____

TOTAL TIME _____

OVEN TEMP _____

INGREDIENTS

_____

_____

_____

_____

_____

_____

_____

DIRECTIONS

_____

_____

_____

_____

_____

_____

_____

_____

INVOCATION

INVOCATION

"SO MOTE IT BE"

RECIPE FOR _____

CULINARY CONCOCTION

CASTING SPELL FOR

_____

SERVES _____

PREP TIME _____

TOTAL TIME _____

OVEN TEMP _____

INGREDIENTS

_____

_____

_____

_____

_____

_____

_____

DIRECTIONS

INVOCATION

INVOCATION

"So Mote It Be"

RECIPE FOR _____

CULINARY CONCOCTION

CASTING SPELL FOR

_____

SERVES _____

PREP TIME _____

TOTAL TIME _____

OVEN TEMP _____

INGREDIENTS

_____

_____

_____

_____

_____

_____

_____

_____

DIRECTIONS

_____

_____

_____

_____

_____

_____

_____

_____

INVOCATION

INVOCATION

"SO MOTE IT BE"

RECIPE FOR _____

CULINARY CONCOCTION

CASTING SPELL FOR

_____

SERVES _____

PREP TIME _____

TOTAL TIME _____

OVEN TEMP _____

INGREDIENTS

_____

_____

_____

_____

_____

_____

_____

_____

DIRECTIONS

_____

_____

_____

_____

_____

_____

_____

_____

INVOCATION

INVOCATION

"SO MOTE IT BE"

RECIPE FOR _____

CULINARY CONCOCTION

CASTING SPELL FOR

_____

SERVES _____

PREP TIME _____

TOTAL TIME _____

OVEN TEMP _____

INGREDIENTS

_____

_____

_____

_____

_____

_____

_____

DIRECTIONS

_____

_____

_____

_____

_____

_____

_____

_____

INVOCATION

INVOCATION

"SO MOTE IT BE"

RECIPE FOR

CULINARY CONCOCTION

CASTING SPELL FOR

_____

SERVES _____

PREP TIME _____

TOTAL TIME _____

OVEN TEMP _____

INGREDIENTS

_____

_____

_____

_____

_____

_____

DIRECTIONS

_____

_____

_____

_____

_____

_____

_____

_____

INVOCATION

INVOCATION

"SO MOTE IT BE"

RECIPE FOR _____

CULINARY CONCOCTION

CASTING SPELL FOR

_____

SERVES _____

PREP TIME _____

TOTAL TIME _____

OVEN TEMP _____

INGREDIENTS

_____

_____

_____

_____

_____

_____

_____

DIRECTIONS

INVOCATION

INVOCATION

"SO MOTE IT BE"

RECIPE FOR _____

CULINARY CONCOCTION

CASTING SPELL FOR

_____

SERVES _____

PREP TIME _____

TOTAL TIME _____

OVEN TEMP _____

INGREDIENTS

_____

_____

_____

_____

_____

_____

_____

DIRECTIONS

_____

_____

_____

_____

_____

_____

_____

_____

INVOCATION

INVOCATION

"So Mote It Be"

RECIPE FOR _____

CULINARY CONCOCTION

CASTING SPELL FOR

_____

SERVES _____

PREP TIME _____

TOTAL TIME _____

OVEN TEMP _____

INGREDIENTS

_____

_____

_____

_____

_____

_____

_____

DIRECTIONS

_____

_____

_____

_____

_____

_____

_____

_____

INVOCATION

INVOCATION

"SO MOTE IT BE"

RECIPE FOR _____

CULINARY CONCOCTION

CASTING SPELL FOR

_____

SERVES _____

PREP TIME _____

TOTAL TIME _____

OVEN TEMP _____

INGREDIENTS

_____

_____

_____

_____

_____

_____

_____

DIRECTIONS

_____

_____

_____

_____

_____

_____

_____

_____

INVOCATION

INVOCATION

"So Mote It Be"

RECIPE FOR _____

CULINARY CONCOCTION

CASTING SPELL FOR

_____

SERVES _____

PREP TIME _____

TOTAL TIME _____

OVEN TEMP _____

INGREDIENTS

_____

_____

_____

_____

_____

_____

_____

DIRECTIONS

_____

_____

_____

_____

_____

_____

_____

_____

INVOCATION

INVOCATION

"SO MOTE IT BE"

RECIPE FOR _____

CULINARY CONCOCTION

CASTING SPELL FOR

_____

SERVES _____

PREP TIME _____

TOTAL TIME _____

OVEN TEMP _____

INGREDIENTS

_____

_____

_____

_____

_____

_____

_____

DIRECTIONS

_____

_____

_____

_____

_____

_____

_____

_____

INVOCATION

INVOCATION

"SO MOTE IT BE"

RECIPE FOR _____

CULINARY CONCOCTION

CASTING SPELL FOR

_____

SERVES _____

PREP TIME _____

TOTAL TIME _____

OVEN TEMP _____

INGREDIENTS

_____

_____

_____

_____

_____

_____

_____

DIRECTIONS

INVOCATION

INVOCATION

"So Mote it Be"

RECIPE FOR _____

CULINARY CONCOCTION

CASTING SPELL FOR

_____

SERVES _____

PREP TIME _____

TOTAL TIME _____

OVEN TEMP _____

INGREDIENTS

_____

_____

_____

_____

_____

_____

_____

DIRECTIONS

INVOCATION

INVOCATION

"SO MOTE IT BE"

RECIPE FOR _____

CULINARY CONCOCTION

CASTING SPELL FOR

_____

SERVES _____

PREP TIME _____

TOTAL TIME _____

OVEN TEMP _____

INGREDIENTS

_____

_____

_____

_____

_____

_____

_____

DIRECTIONS

INVOCATION

INVOCATION

"So Mote It Be"

RECIPE FOR _____

CULINARY CONCOCTION

CASTING SPELL FOR

_____

SERVES _____

PREP TIME _____

TOTAL TIME _____

OVEN TEMP _____

INGREDIENTS

_____

_____

_____

_____

_____

_____

_____

DIRECTIONS

INVOCATION

INVOCATION

"So Mote It Be"

RECIPE FOR

CULINARY CONCOCTION

CASTING SPELL FOR

SERVES

PREP TIME

TOTAL TIME

OVEN TEMP

INGREDIENTS

DIRECTIONS

INVOCATION

INVOCATION

"So Mote It Be"

RECIPE FOR

CULINARY CONCOCTION

CASTING SPELL FOR

SERVES
PREP TIME
TOTAL TIME
OVEN TEMP

INGREDIENTS

DIRECTIONS

INVOCATION

INVOCATION

"SO MOTE IT BE"

RECIPE FOR _____

CULINARY CONCOCTION

CASTING SPELL FOR

_____

SERVES _____

PREP TIME _____

TOTAL TIME _____

OVEN TEMP _____

INGREDIENTS

_____

_____

_____

_____

_____

_____

_____

DIRECTIONS

_____

_____

_____

_____

_____

_____

_____

_____

INVOCATION

INVOCATION

"SO MOTE IT BE"

RECIPE FOR _____

CULINARY CONCOCTION

CASTING SPELL FOR

_____

SERVES _____

PREP TIME _____

TOTAL TIME _____

OVEN TEMP _____

INGREDIENTS

_____

_____

_____

_____

_____

_____

_____

_____

DIRECTIONS

INVOCATION

INVOCATION

"SO MOTE IT BE"

RECIPE FOR _____

CULINARY CONCOCTION

CASTING SPELL FOR

_____

SERVES _____

PREP TIME _____

TOTAL TIME _____

OVEN TEMP _____

INGREDIENTS

_____

_____

_____

_____

_____

_____

_____

DIRECTIONS

INVOCATION

INVOCATION

"SO MOTE IT BE"

RECIPE FOR _____

CULINARY CONCOCTION

CASTING SPELL FOR

_____

SERVES _____

PREP TIME _____

TOTAL TIME _____

OVEN TEMP _____

INGREDIENTS

_____

_____

_____

_____

_____

_____

_____

DIRECTIONS

INVOCATION

INVOCATION

"SO MOTE IT BE"

RECIPE FOR _____

CULINARY CONCOCTION

CASTING SPELL FOR

_____

SERVES _____

PREP TIME _____

TOTAL TIME _____

OVEN TEMP _____

INGREDIENTS

_____
_____
_____
_____
_____
_____
_____

DIRECTIONS

_____
_____
_____
_____
_____
_____
_____
_____

INVOCATION

INVOCATION

"SO MOTE IT BE"

RECIPE FOR _____

CULINARY CONCOCTION

CASTING SPELL FOR

_____

SERVES _____

PREP TIME _____

TOTAL TIME _____

OVEN TEMP _____

INGREDIENTS

_____

_____

_____

_____

_____

_____

DIRECTIONS

_____

_____

_____

_____

_____

_____

_____

_____

INVOCATION

INVOCATION

"SO MOTE IT BE"

RECIPE FOR _____

CULINARY CONCOCTION

CASTING SPELL FOR

_____

SERVES _____

PREP TIME _____

TOTAL TIME _____

OVEN TEMP _____

INGREDIENTS

_____

_____

_____

_____

_____

_____

DIRECTIONS

INVOCATION

INVOCATION

"SO MOTE IT BE"

RECIPE FOR _____

CULINARY CONCOCTION

CASTING SPELL FOR

_____

SERVES _____

PREP TIME _____

TOTAL TIME _____

OVEN TEMP _____

INGREDIENTS

_____

_____

_____

_____

_____

_____

_____

DIRECTIONS

INVOCATION

INVOCATION

"SO MOTE IT BE"

RECIPE FOR _____

CULINARY CONCOCTION

CASTING SPELL FOR

_____

SERVES _____

PREP TIME _____

TOTAL TIME _____

OVEN TEMP _____

INGREDIENTS

_____

_____

_____

_____

_____

_____

_____

DIRECTIONS

INVOCATION

INVOCATION

"SO MOTE IT BE"

RECIPE FOR _____

CULINARY CONCOCTION

CASTING SPELL FOR

_____

SERVES _____

PREP TIME _____

TOTAL TIME _____

OVEN TEMP _____

INGREDIENTS

_____

_____

_____

_____

_____

_____

_____

DIRECTIONS

_____

_____

_____

_____

_____

_____

_____

_____

INVOCATION

INVOCATION

"SO MOTE IT BE"

RECIPE FOR _____

CULINARY CONCOCTION

CASTING SPELL FOR

_____

SERVES _____

PREP TIME _____

TOTAL TIME _____

OVEN TEMP _____

INGREDIENTS

_____

_____

_____

_____

_____

_____

_____

DIRECTIONS

INVOCATION

INVOCATION

"SO MOTE IT BE"

RECIPE FOR _____

CULINARY CONCOCTION

CASTING SPELL FOR

_____

SERVES _____

PREP TIME _____

TOTAL TIME _____

OVEN TEMP _____

INGREDIENTS

_____

_____

_____

_____

_____

_____

_____

DIRECTIONS

_____

_____

_____

_____

_____

_____

_____

_____

INVOCATION

INVOCATION

"SO MOTE IT BE"

RECIPE FOR _____

CULINARY CONCOCTION

CASTING SPELL FOR

_____

SERVES _____

PREP TIME _____

TOTAL TIME _____

OVEN TEMP _____

INGREDIENTS

_____

_____

_____

_____

_____

_____

_____

DIRECTIONS

INVOCATION

INVOCATION

"SO MOTE IT BE"

RECIPE FOR _____

CULINARY CONCOCTION

CASTING SPELL FOR

_____

SERVES _____

PREP TIME _____

TOTAL TIME _____

OVEN TEMP _____

INGREDIENTS

_____

_____

_____

_____

_____

_____

DIRECTIONS

_____

_____

_____

_____

_____

_____

_____

_____

INVOCATION

INVOCATION

"So Mote It Be"

The Good Luck Kitchen Witch

Nothing spills
Nothing spoils
Overcooks or overboils
This kitchen witch upon her broom
Brings love and luck to any room!

www.ingramcontent.com/pod-product-compliance
Lightning Source LLC
Chambersburg PA
CBHW081331090426
42737CB00017B/3090